Signal Reactions

AND OTHER POEMS

Language in Action Series

Martin H. Levinson
Photography by Katherine Liepe-Levinson

INSTITUTE OF GENERAL SEMANTICS

Signal Reactions and Other Poems

Copyright © 2020 by Martin Levinson

Published by the Institute of General Semantics
72-11 Austin Street, #233
Forest Hills, New York, 11375
www.generalsemantics.org

Cover Design by Katherine Liepe-Levinson
www.katherineliepelevinson.zenfolio

Interior Book Design by Scribe Freelance
www.scribefreelance.com

ISBN: 978-1-970164-04-6 (Paperback)
978-1-970164-05-3 (eBook)

LIBRARY OF CONGRESS CATALOGING-IN-PUBLICATION DATA

Names: Levinson, Martin H., 1946- author / Liepe-Levinson, Katherine, 1953- illustrator.
Title: Signal reactions and other poems / Martin H. Levinson.
Description: [New York] : [Institute of General Semantics], [2020] |
Identifiers: LCCN 2020016457 (print) | LCCN 2020016458 (ebook) |
ISBN
  9781970164046 (paperback) | ISBN 9781970164053 (ebook)
Subjects: LCSH: General semantics—Poetry. | LCGFT: Poetry.
Classification: LCC PS3612.E9287 S54 2020 (print) | LCC PS3612.
E9287
  (ebook) | DDC 811/.6—dc23
LC record available at https://lccn.loc.gov/2020016457
LC ebook record available at https://lccn.loc.gov/2020016458

Poetry often conveys in a few sentences more of lasting value than a whole volume of scientific analysis.
—ALFRED KORZYBSKI

The **Language in Action** series, sponsored by the Institute of General Semantics, publishes books devoted to creative modes of expression that can open the doors of perception, and foster better understandings of the nature of language, symbols, communication, and the semantic, technological, and media environments that we inhabit. Through processes of play and probing, art can bring into awareness alternative forms of experience and evaluation to the everyday, routine, taken-for-granted world. It can also shed new light on mind and method, consciousness and culture, abstracting and attention, ecology and enlightenment, and, most important to students of general semantics, science and sanity.

Founded in 1938 by Alfred Korzybski, the Institute of General Semantics promotes, in the words of S.I. Hayakawa, *the study of how not be a damn fool*. As a non-aristotelian system devoted to enhancing human potential, general semantics has inspired numerous novelists, poets, artists, musicians, and creative thinkers. General semantics today is devoted to explorations of meaning and the meaning of meaning, of metaphors and memes, archetypes and arts, symbols and signals, signs and significance, codes and ciphers, sense perception and sense-making, and the vast variety of ways of seeing, feeling, and thinking that humanity is heir to. The quarterly journal of the IGS, *ETC: A Review of General Semantics*, has been publishing essays, research, and literary work since 1943.

Acknowledgments

Thank you: to Lance Strate, the editor of this series, and the Institute of General Semantics for providing a way for these poems to get out into the wider world; to Matthew Lippman for helping me to select the poems that are included in this book; to my wife, Katherine Liepe-Levinson, for agreeing to illustrate the book with her amazing photographs and for all her encouragement over the years on writing projects; to the members of the Westhampton Free Library Writers Group for their cogent comments and critiques on many of these poems; to Donna Lee McGullum for her superb editing job on this book; and to the editors of the following journals where these poems first appeared:

- *Artifact Nouveau*: "The Dusky Red Wine Stain," "Sturm und Drang"
- *Avocet: A Journal of Nature Poems*: "Summer's End"
- *Bards Annual*: "Cock Tale"
- *The Bitchin' Kitsch*: "Goodness in the Gilded Age"
- *BRICKrhetoric*: "Brooklyn 1957"
- *Broad River Review*: "Along the Peconic"
- *The Broken Plate*: "The Thief"
- *Buckoff Literary Magazine*: "Is Everybody Happy?"
- *Canary Literary Magazine*: "Every Day is Earth Day"
- *Carnival Literary Magazine*: "Say What?"
- *Chronogram*: "Labels"
- *The Coe Review*: "It's All Tangled Up Over There"
- *Common Ground Review*: "The Penitent Sea"
- *Eunoia Review*: "Where It's @"
- *ETC: A Review of General Semantics*: "Ode to the Structural Differential"
- *First Literary Review East*: "Double Dating," "Thesis, Antithesis, Synthesis," "This is the Way the World Ends"
- *Freshet*: "In the Borough of Queens"
- *Freshwater Literary Journal*: "On Reaching Seventy"
- *Hello Poetry*: "Who's Listening," "How Do I Love Thee . . ."

- *Literary Mama*: "Carpe Diem"
- *Magazine of Arts & Humanities*: "Covid-19"
- *Mobius*: "Aristotle's Ideal City"
- *Musings*: "The Way of Things"
- *Occupoetry*: "Song of My Selfie"
- *Offcourse Literary Journal*: "Singular Dudes," "Connections," "America the Beautiful"
- *Otoliths*: "C'est la Vie"
- *New Verse News*: "Nine Dead in Dayton"
- *Parody Poetry Journal*: "Ode to Dorothy Parker"
- *Penumbra*: "Penumbras"
- *The Poet's Art*: "Lost in Thought," "Making Contact"
- *Potomac Review*: "A Mammoth Lamentation"
- *The Prompt Literary Magazine*: "I Am Not an MRI Machine"
- *Rattle*: "Gilly Gilly Ossenfeffer Katzenellenbogen by the Sea"
- *Reflections in Poetry and Prose*: "Rock Around the Clock"
- *SAMSHA Peerlink*: "My Mother My Coach"
- *Serving House Journal*: "Corrections"
- *South Florida Poetry Journal*: "In Search of Lost Time"
- *Spank the Carp*: "Clarity Kills," "First Thought, Best Thought," "Rally 'Round the Flag"
- *Specter Magazine*: "A Horoscope Prediction for the Goddess That You Are"
- *Third Wednesday*: "Marriage Metaphysics," "The Most Exasperated Person in America"
- *Time-Binding*: "Global Madness," "Be a Man"
- *Verse Virtual*: "Wish Me Good Luck," "The Formula $E=mc^2$," "Procrastination Blues"
- *Vietnam War Poetry*: "Sunday on a Bench"
- *Winamop*: "Signal Reactions," "I am an Iceberg"

For Kathy

Contents

Preface

THE TITLE OF this book, *Signal Reactions*, refers to a general semantics (GS) term signifying an instant, unthinking, subjective response to a person, place, thing, or event. These responses rarely work out well but they are so instinctive it is hard to resist them. Delaying our reactions gives us time to think about what is going on in situations, which can help us to respond more effectively. Some examples of signal and delayed reactions can be seen in my poems "The Most Exasperated Person in America" (p. 93) and "Summer's End" (pp. 139-140).

Poetry is largely about mapping one's inner-world responses—thoughts, sensations, emotions, etc. My inner world tends toward seeing the absurdity in life and rather than keeping those assessments to myself I often write poetry: sublimation through cogitation.

The poems in this book are grouped into four categories: "The Human Comedy," "Love," "America," and "Mind and Nature." Of course, as in life, there is overlap among categorical classifications. Feel free to skip from one section to another, or read the poems in reverse order, or read the poems on the even pages first, or come up with some other way to read the poems. The choice is yours and I thank you for making the effort.

Photographer's Note

AS A FORMER professional dancer, I am frequently asked why my focus is on photography (often thought of as a "static" art), rather than on video and film (which appear to be movement-based). In *Science and Sanity*, Alfred Korzybski encourages his readers to examine the individual fixed frames that make up moving pictures. For Korzybski, "arresting" the mind-boggling stream of events in a film to contemplate each image one by one allows us the time to investigate and analyze the specifics of every frame as we are looking at them—instead of trying to grasp or remember them as the movie flashes by.[1] For me, a photograph offers contemplation, and thus a personal experience that is more active and on-going.

Like much of poetry, a photograph reveals a decisive, particular moment or experience. Despite the science and technology involved in camera work, photography is as subjective as poetry—no two photographers can capture exactly the same image (nor would most wish to). Both the poet and the photographer labor over processing their works using color, contrast, dynamic range, rhythm/repetition, shape, and tone to name a few. Poets paint with words; photographers paint with light.

One of the joys of studying Korzybski's general semantics is that the practice is not limited to how words and symbols produce meaning, but also how meaning is produced and evaluated through all our senses.

I was delighted and honored that Marty asked me to contribute my photographs to *Signal Reactions*. The goal was not to visually illustrate his poems with my images but to complement and sometimes converse with them. Many thanks to Lance Strate, who edits this series, and to the Institute of General Semantics for encouraging and sponsoring such projects.

---

1 Alfred Korzybski, *Science and Sanity: An Introduction to Non-Aristotelian Systems and General Semantics, 5th edition* (Fort Worth, TX: Institute of General Semantics, 1995), 235, 292, 578.

Crossing

Signal Reactions

Red light,
Don't Walk,
thoughts of
being tied to
a desk with no
window,
Stop, Look,
listen to a
loudmouth
screaming
next to me
into his phone.

Red light,
Don't Talk
about a
home I've
outgrown,
friends
who keep
me frozen
to the curb.

Signal changes.

I move forward.

Barreling down a
boulevard of broken
dreams and bootless
bustle like hooligan
hotrods from hell,
forces threaten to
kill and maim me
if I cross the
thoroughfare.

I cross anyway.

THE HUMAN COMEDY

Happier than Me

Is Everybody Happy?

There is no algorithm for happiness
but I ask Siri anyway. She replies,
surveys say Switzerland is the happiest
country in the world, not sure why, could
be the chocolate, maybe it's the cheese.

Buddhists say to attain contentment
one must overcome cravings for
iPhones, Patek Philippe watches, BMWs,
and early bird dinners served until six.

Scientists have the ability to
measure happiness but not as
well as novelists, poets, and my
ninety-five-year-old mother.

Happiness is the only thing
humans desire for its own sake,
said Aristotle, to which Thoreau
replied: joy is like a butterfly,
the more you chase it, the more
it will elude you.

For Linus, happiness is a
warm blanket. For me,
it's a toasted bagel with
peanut butter, jelly,
cup of coffee on the side.

Selfie Nation

In Search of Lost Time

Sipping a peppermint white chocolate
  mocha and eating a Greek yogurt parfait
@ Starbucks Tammy tweets me at the
  same time Tommy texts *JLo just strolled*
by me on the sidewalk where everyone is

  taking selfies, sending messages,
listening to podcasts that don't contain
  the fact that Felicia broke up with Felipe,
which I learned from Phaedra on Facebook
  who suggested I link-surf Wikipedia,

binge-watch *Game of Thrones*, share images
  on Instagram of last night's imbroglio
that I snapped with my iPhone XR, a
  gadget with a gazillion uses held together
by gravity, dark matter, and a belief that

  boredom and stagnation can be beaten by
Google and PlayStation while doing the
  Times crossword on my MacBook Pro
where I am seeking to answer the question

how did people before the digital age live
  without YouTube.

Rain Man

Carpe Diem

Dad was never the same
after being forced to retire
at age sixty-three;
travel, OTB, playing
the market, watching
Jeopardy—not like
running a big company;
less pay, less perks,
less I'm the man,
who are you?

Mom tried to
buck him up:
having folks over,
restaurant meals,
not napping in the
passenger seat on car
rides from New York
to Florida. All bupkis.
Thirty years of pouting
and putzing then
Parkinson's did him in.

Because he was a vet
mom was able to get
an army color guard
at his funeral and
after the service
they gave her our
nation's flag: My
country 'tis of thee
Depressed retiree
Of thee I sing.

Michelangelo painted
frescoes at the Vatican

chapel at age eighty-nine.
Benjamin Franklin invented
bifocals when he was
seventy-eight. The Delany
sisters wrote a book titled
*Having Our Say: The
Delany Sisters' First 100 Years.*
My father never read it.

By the Sea

Gilly Gilly Ossenfeffer
Katzenellenbogen by the Sea

Where is Gilly Gilly Ossenfeffer Katzenellenbogen
   she said
as we motored down the Long Island Expressway
   and I said
where is it written that I have to
   answer your crazy questions
   and she said
where did I put my makeup case and mascara
   and I said
where did I go so wrong in life that I have to
   constantly listen to a woman talking to herself
   and she said
where is the pretzel stick that I gave you to
   save for me this morning
   and I said
where is the nearest insane asylum I can
   drive you to so you can get treated
   and she said
where do you get off talking to me like that
   and I said
where do you think you are, in a chauffeured limousine
   with a driver who will cater to your every whim
   and she said
where can I hit you that will leave no marks
   and not cause us to crash
   and I said
where are the quarters I left in the glove compartment
   to pay for parking meters
   and she said
where oh where have his little coins gone
   oh where oh where can they be
   and I said
where they are is where I put them unless
   someone placed them somewhere else

and she said
where do you think that would be, Sherlock
and I said
where do you think a person who doesn't care
 about taking things would lay the money
and she said
where the hell are we
and I said
where we have always been
and she said
where is that
and I said
where that is is for me to know
 and you to find out
and she said
where is the next rest stop
 I need to get out of the car
and I said
where can a guy go to
 get some peace around here
and she said
where there are no human beings around
 like Mars
and I said
where did we go off the rails
 on this trip
and she said
where we went off was when
 we met ten years ago
and I said
where do you think you'll be
 ten years from now
and she said
where I can wake up happy
 and not be bothered by you
and I said
where exactly do you think
 that would be
and she said
Gilly Gilly Ossenfeffer Katzenellenbogen
 by the Sea.

Day Trader

Corrections

The stock market needs a
  correction and so do kids
    who yell at their mothers for

more cake love, take love
  wherever you can find it on
    the fifth-largest planet in a

solar system full of people
  carting emotional baggage
    with stickers reading fucked up

at birth, mom liked you better,
  dad ignored me, I should have
    majored in business, and the

humanity, oh the humanity,
  rushing from pillar to Post-it
    notes saying bring home

eggs, pay the doctor, pay the
  plumber, pay what you can
    and eat lots of bran so you

can be regular and fit in
  with the crowd on the
    Fourth of July munching

hot dogs, drinking beer,
  watching fireworks explode
    inside your head from the

stress you've been having
  at the office and at home
    that makes you wish you could

pull a Gauguin and go to Tahiti,
  which is not the answer because
    you'd be bored out of your gourd

walking the beaches each day
  looking for loose change and
    loose women to talk to and maybe

mess around with a little bit
  but not too much since then
    you wouldn't have the strength

to check your portfolio to try
  to figure out how to not get
    slammed by forces beyond

your control.

Turn It OFF!

The Thief

He sits silent in my living room
daring me to press his buttons so
he can burble and babble his sweet
talk to transfix my attention. I vow

to resist my urge to turn on,
tune in, watch. Not now, pal.
There are books that need to be
read, emails that need to be sent,

floors that need to be cleaned, bills
that need to be paid, thoughts that
need to be reflected on in quiet
solitude without the blare of the

putative news of the day, commercial
cackle, and whatever shows lurk on
my DVR. Just give me five minutes he
tells me telepathically and sucker that I am

I grant the crook his wish and click
the remote and five gets you ten
and ten gets you twenty and twenty
gets you forty and before you know it

there goes the evening and it's
such a crime that once again
I've been duped by this cunning
thief of time.

End of the Line

Ode to Dorothy Parker

Peanuts can kill you;
Wheat can make you sick;
Shellfish can ill you;
And steak sits like a brick.
Lettuce carries parasites;
Onions make you cry;
Coffee keeps you up at night;
You might as well die.

What For?

Be a Man

Be a man she said,
and I can but what for,
being a man is such a
damn bore, I'd rather
wimp out and be a
complainer; whining's
cathartic, for health a
no brainer.

So, my boss doesn't like
the clothes that I wear,
and my backstabbing
colleagues do not play fair,
and it's either too hot or
it's either too cold, and
and it sucked being young
and who wants to be old,

and the house is a mess that
we really must clean, and Jimmy
our neighbor is incredibly mean,
and the kids don't appreciate
meals that you make, and when
we have sex why do you get to fake,

and I detest Jane and I detest Lee,
and I loathe when detesting them
you don't agree, and I can't
understand why I have to drive, and
you get to text and rest and revive,

and I saw the red light and the car
that cut in, and the warnings you
give me get under my skin, and
when we go out can you please
not be late, and pray do not tell me

you'll just have to wait,

and I could simply go on
spewing demands, and
wouldn't you know it,
that's just like a man.

Virtually Speaking

Where It's @

No one really knows
how it first started out,
that thing called the *snail*
by Italians, the sine qua non
of internet communication
whose obscurity ended in '71
when a techie teletyped a
message to himself in
Cambridge Mass. using
the graceful curlicue on
top of the two.

With that message @
became where it's at for
electronically connecting
to humans or facsimiles
thereof and hallelujah, no
more phone conversations
or getting together with
mundane mortals which
means breakups can be
done via Facebook and
Twitter, your pain can be
posted on Instagram, your
anguish can be blogged,

you and your ex can be
alone together with
righteous illusions about
who was to blame, how
things should have been.

Metropolis

Aristotle's Ideal City

A city, like a person,
needs internal goodness and
wisdom in order to be happy.
            —Aristotle's *Politics*, Book VII

The muggers like the cops,
   the loonies like the docs,
blacks like whites and whites
   like blacks and browns and
reds and it is said the judges
   can't be bought, the politicians
take no bribes, products come
   with guarantees, taxi rides are
mostly free, as is health care
   for the poor, top-notch teaching
de rigueur, virtue, goodness
   everywhere, I dig this poem,
it lacks despair, fair's not foul,
   foul's fair, no smell of garbage in
the air, trash picked up every day,
   at court the folks have equal say,
on the street the fat is chewed,
   people bonding is pursued,
Dom got married, Jane is sick,
   Mark's kid's learning magic tricks,
a polis filled with pride,
   imagined in my head, Aristotle
would have loved this place,
   but Aristotle's dead.

No Travelers

Global Madness

Pakistan, Afghanistan, Baluchistan
Are in a jam.
Kazakhstan, Turkmenistan, Uzbekistan
Are on the lam.

Colombia, Bulgaria, Zambia, Abkhazia
It seems like I am getting crazier and crazier.
Mongolia, Estonia, Malaysia, Mauritania
The doctor says I'm suffering from geographic mania.

Mali, Malawi, Fiji, Burundi
This medicine is making me feel kind of funny.
Iceland, Switzerland, Swaziland, Somaliland
Can anybody tell me what happened to my wristband?

Malta, Cuba, Canada, Ghana
I'd like to find out who stole my banana.
Mexico, Monaco, Morocco, Montenegro
I hope I'm not developing a bad case of lumbago.

Germany, Italy, Hungary, Turkey
This stuff that I have written seems weird and quite quirky.
Norway, Paraguay, Palau, Vatican City
James Thurber lives and I'm Walter Mitty.

Too Late

Procrastination Blues

Showing up punctually is
not a possibility when what
should've been done the
day before is being done

right before we head out to
fill-in-the-blank, we're on the
road, making calls, the cat
threw up, the traffic's bad,

climate change is not a hoax
but if it was we'd still be late
for parties, the theater, the
flight we missed to Florida,

the cab was there, the roads were
clear, four hours prep was not
enough to board the plane to
Delray Beach, Flamingo Punch,

a poolside lunch, sitting in an
airport lounge, where's your
cellphone, dresser drawer,
fully charged, mine's there too,

let's go home, have a beer,
tomorrow get our ass in gear.

Sardines

Clarity Kills

Clarity kills good art by devaluing the
difficulty needed to apprehend the praxis
of prosody in a quotationist, citationist,
double-coded, mannered, oblique,
post-modern world.

Lucidity is not for literary luminaries
but for literary losers who can
only express themselves in ways
to be understood.

Mediate
      obfuscate
equivocate
      expostulate
vitiate
      germinate
amalgamate
      attenuate

but please

don't prate prose
whose   meanings
are   too   readily
dis   closed.

Have a Nice Day

Say What?

I.

Say *have a nice day* you'll be taken to task
for not saying a great day or one that's a blast,
whatever you say may be misconstrued so
say precious little, merci beaucoup.

II.

To put words in writing is palpably worse than
talking to people and here is the curse, when you
write something down farewell the excuse, you
misheard heard what I said, those aren't my views.

III.

Nonverbal messages shun and negate, they
confuse other humans which isn't so great,
stay stiff as a board when speaking with others
except in the case if those others are lovers.

IV.

To downgrade the chances of being misread
die and have people connect with you dead,
but beware this device is subject to fail, for
they say in forensics the dead can tell tales.

Civility

Cock Tale

I bite my lips, pinch my thighs,
pray I don't throw myself off the
twenty-first floor terrace we are
standing on as you sip your scotch
and soda, chomp on a cigar,

pontificate over nuclear
proliferation, climate change,
the lack of civility in everyday life
and your aching feet that I want to
stomp on each time you say

what is this world coming to,
politicians are liars and crooks,
bring back the good old days,
as if I don't know I want to
disappear and become a

Trappist monk obeying
a vow of silence with my
fellow monks who don't talk
but love each other because
how can you not love someone

who doesn't bore you to death
or make you want to kill them
with their washed-out platitudes
and monochromatic conversation
that dye Technicolor discussions

dull and dreary gray.

LOVE

Flying High

Penumbras

When two penumbras overlap
their shadows attract
and merge
swell and surge toward
one another like

you and me,
opaque objects
overlaid with desire
to connect and grow
beyond separate silhouettes.

But we're scared to reveal
what down deep
we feel so
hemming and hawing
we search for

predawn rays of
I dig your smile
that's a nice dress
you're such a good dancer
you move very well.

Then passing between
the sun
and the moon
we avert an eclipse,
we light up the room.

Rough Landing Ahead

Sturm und Drang

The weather in the
      living room is bad,
drenching mockery,
      claps of ridicule,
derision and contempt.

My insides are
      icing up from
the cold stares
      I'm getting,
flaps are stuck
      saying sorry.

Shouldn't have
      called you lame
when you told me
      to get a life,
should have just
      thought it.

Body's shaking,
      big mouth's buckled,
clemency gauge
      reading zero.

Looks like a
      rough landing with
a long layover for
      repairs before we
can fly again.

Matched Pair

Double Dating

I love you
You love me
You love you
I love me too.

Undecided

I am an I
      c
       e
        b
         e
          r
           g

I am an iceberg
floating in
the Sea of
Indecisiveness,
hidden motives
deep beneath
the surface,
jagged peaks
of reason
and despair.
Ambiguity
is rock solid,
a mile thick,
algae and
confidence
nowhere
to be seen.
Go with the
floe I tell
myself,
melting from
the strain of
trying to
ask you out.
If I succeed
in doing that
you might
say no.

We Are and Are Not

Marriage Metaphysics

One cannot say of something that it is
         and that it is not at the same time said
Aristotle in his *Metaphysics,* which
         people foolishly believed despite

knowing you can hate and love someone
         at the identical moment they tell you
they wrecked your car and beg your
         forgiveness, especially if that person is

your wife who has access to all your
         money and emotions that you thought
you controlled but really don't because
         your amygdala keeps hijacking signals

that should be sent to your neocortex for
         analysis whenever your spouse yells at you
or claims it was your fault she was late in
         leaving the house because you kept looking

at your watch which made her nervous
         so she put on the wrong outfit
that she then had to change when she
         realized the mistake, which is something

you don't have to worry about because
         you don't care how you look and you
could have fed the cats while she was
         getting dressed and now she'll have to

do it because you're not concerned about living
         things as much as she is and all you're
interested in is getting to the goddamned theater
         before the curtain goes up and it's

probably a lousy show anyway but she's going
         with you because you wanted to see it and
she promised you she would go and she's sorry
         about being late and owes you one and

she'll take care of getting the car fixed.

Unknown Goddess of the Wherehouse

A Horoscope Prediction for the Goddess That You Are

On coupon-Wednesday you will meet
the man of your dreams at the deli counter.

He'll be cloaked in a classy white uniform
and papier-mâché hat.

Smile demurely at this sexy supermarket chevalier

and ask what he would suggest for people who
love cold cuts like liverwurst. If he replies

I don't give advice on
matters like that, I just slice the meat
the way the customer tells me to

he's the wrong guy.
It's the fellow next to him.

I am Not a Camera

I Am Not an MRI Machine

To say I can see through you implies
        in some weird way
                that I am a radiologic voyeur

able to reconnoiter your inner recesses
        to visualize detailed pictures
                of your thoughts and feelings

without having you lie on an analyst's couch
        where a rotating history of
                your life is used to scan

powerful early influences that
        provide three-D data on your
                psychological growth to create

an image of how you became
        the person you are today with your
                magnetic flaws, atomic strengths,

and the contrasts they produce.

At Bat

Making Contact

She says she can't get a word in
  edgewise, which may be true, but
if she's calling the conversational
  balls and strikes how can she

simultaneously be up at the plate
  waiting for a curveball she thinks
I'm going to throw her when I
  haven't decided what pitch to fling

to the catcher sitting in my skull,
  who's motioning for a fast ball,
which may not be the best idea,
  as she may be looking for a heater

she can hit out of the ballpark and
  into the parking lot where we're
sitting in a car and I'm pondering
  whether to lob a change of pace

and ask her to forgive me for
  being such a lousy listener.

Double Jeopardy

The Dusky Red Wine Stain

The dusky red wine stain
laughs at me, mocks my efforts
to erase its existence from our
white featherbed where I spilled

my drink after you told me don't
imbibe in the boudoir because the
Johnstown Flood, 9/11, and the
Triangle Fire disaster could

have been prevented if people
had stayed in the kitchen with
their libations and not wandered
through the house with crimson

colored liquids that when freed from
their containers do indelible harm
to furniture and relationships
which need to be carefully tended

to keep their sheen from turning shabby
like the Andersons across the street,
split up after fifty years because
he cracked her vintage glass coffee

table with his fishing gear, and the
La-Z-Boy recliner in our den, which
I should have guarded but didn't so
the cat clawed through its cloth cover

that I can't reverse time to undo, keep
the Hindenburg from flying, hold
Challenger on the ground, steer
Titanic 'round the berg, unpour

a glass of ruby red wine.

Promises in the Park

How Do I Love Thee . . .

My love for you is like an
   IPO yearning to gain traction,
a center of excellence, an

industry model hoping to get
   to the next level by incentivizing
you to think outside the box and

view me as a white knight who
   brings to the table seamless
adoration and customer service

dedication to disambiguate your
   every desire, set the night on fire,
and roll out the best damn omelet

you've ever tasted when we
   ramp up in the morning.

Soul Mates

Singular Dudes

Pooch is a butting, rubbing, pushing,
    pawing, I-want-some-of that-cake kind of
cat who lets me stroke his whiskers and
    pet his wavy marcel coat for as long as
and strong as I'd like.

When he stares at me with his slanty
    yellowish-devilish green eyes I get
the feeling someone's home in his
    tabby cranium, that I'm viewed
not merely as a hominid meal ticket
    but as a beasty chum worthy of slurping
and burping beer from a bowl.

Buddy, his younger feline companion,
    is a cat of a different color, a fearful mouser
who after nine years of being faithfully fed,
    dutifully taken care of, sees me as a stranger
in the kingdom of carnivores and a source of
    continuous bafflement and bemusement.

No going to the bar with Bud for wet food,
    ale, and the camaraderie of life forms
banging heads together. No going to the
    couch for a kneading session, plop down
and restorative nap. No bounding through
    the house bumping up against each other,

but instead
a gentle extension
of a hand for sniffing,
a beseeching
dulcet voice,
a tremulous query,
what can I do
to make you like me?

Seeking Shelter

In the Borough of Queens

I am an immigrant from the
Republic of Loneliness and
Solitude seeking connection
and shelter on a cold winter's
eve in the borough of Queens
where Asians, Russians,
Colombians, Greeks,
a mighty swirl of
divergent people,
banded together,
searching for love in
Flushing tearooms,
Whitestone taverns,
Jackson Heights bodegas,
Astoria cafés, looking for

what we have tonight in your
Kew Gardens apartment across from
Ben's Bagel Stop on Union Turnpike,
next to a 7-11 open 24/7.

Under stars that can't be seen,
the city skyline glows distant
through your twelfth-floor
bedroom window,

a dog barks, sirens can be heard, a
drunk shouts loudly on the street below
but not as loudly as us, two lovers
naked under the covers,
laughing and screaming.

Grid

Connections

My nonagenarian paterfamilias sits
on a green cloth recliner watching
television, remote in one hand,

pen in the other, doing the Sunday
Times crossword puzzle while
listening to WABC talk radio

and yelling for my mother to
bring him an apple and the cup of
hot tea he's been waiting for

for the last ten years which is
not as long as he's been asking
that a TV be connected in his

bedroom so he can watch the
latest market updates on the
Bloomberg Business Channel

and bushwa on FOX News that
my wife can't stand but she
views it with my father who

bugs her about being a lefty
who understands nothing of
the world but something about

technology which she puts into
practice when she sets him up on
Skype, downloads his phone bills,

types out his emails, connects the
television in my parents' boudoir
that I bought but don't know how to

install but she does, and will do,
because the family grid is
important to her.

Let No One Put Asunder

The Way of Things

Water hardens
into hoarfrost
dewdrops form
on grass at dawn,

bears take naps
throughout the winter
bees swarm when
the weather's warm,

sweet corn grows in
summer seasons
leaves fall off
autumnal trees,

clouds develop
out of nowhere
sea tides wax
then they recede,

nature changes
as does nurture
that's the way
it's meant to be,

yet I will love you
you will love me
always and
unceasingly.

Heart of a Rose

My Mother My Coach

When I was twelve I went
  into a batting slump, cried
    myself to sleep at night,
      didn't eat, thought I was a

totally worthless human
  being because I couldn't
    hit a pink rubber ball with
      a sawed-off broom handle.

Told my mother who agreed
  to throw me rolled-up balls
    of socks in the living room,
      after school, before my

father came home. Lamps
  fell, I knocked the aerial off
    the TV, sent roses and knick-knacks
      flying, got picked first in the

choose-up games on the block
  because my mom was not a lady
    who lunched or a furniture queen
      but someone who cared about

what was going on in the mind of
  a stressed-out kid who loved Duke
    Snider, the Brooklyn Dodgers,
      and other baseball stuff she knew

nothing about except
  it made her son happy.

AMERICA

Lift the Lamp

Song of My Selfie

I hear America singing, the varied voices I hear,

Those of stockbrokers, each one singing buy low,
       sell high.
The attorneys, chanting in Latin as they clog up the
          court system with ludicrous litigation to
               extract exorbitant fees.
The medical insurance companies, humming while
          they raise their premiums and deny your
              claim for a dental cleaning.
The avaricious tune of the CEO, crying I deserve a
          bonus even though my business went bust.
The siren song of the public relations flack,
          tooting the praises of coal, oil, and
             toxic chemicals.
The banker, whistling all the way to the bank that has
          been bailed out with taxpayer largesse.
The covetous credit card companies, crooning take on
          debt you can't afford and don't pay now,
             pay later at usurious rates of interest.
The politicians, purring sweet nothings as they
          block legislation to ease our nation's woes.

Each singing what belongs to
          him or her and to no one else.
Each singing for their supper,
          and for your dinner too.

Nowhere to Go

The Most Exasperated Person in America

Lines to buy this
  lines to buy that which
I need but don't want to
  wait for my stomach signals
 as it churns and acidifies
  my low frustration tolerance
that has me thinking if this
  traffic does not move soon I
will go postal and crunch my
  car into the eighteen-wheeler
ahead of me which is blocking
  my view of this road to nowhere
that is only good to drive on
  stoned or at two in the morning
when proper little motorists are
  in bed and not clogging the
thoroughfares with their excrescent
  presence and inane automobiles that
keeps me from getting to point A from
  point B the point being maybe I should
go to the country where I would not have
  to put up with this mechanized mob
that is driving me to distraction as I
  wait endlessly on the phone for an
impossible to understand operator in some
  developing country to handle a simple
 request for a copy of my last month's
  electric bill that I lack because my
home computer crashed and nothing was
  backed up so my life is basically over
but I want to pay what I owe because
  I am not a bad person just a beaten biped
trying his best to get through this vale of
  tears and the traffic that has had me
trapped for the last three hours which if it
  does not ease up shortly will lead me to
ditch my clothes, climb onto the roof of
  my Camry, cup my hands to my mouth,
and scream like a demented out of control
  mother-trucker all the way to China.

Jungle Gym in Tel Aviv

It's All Tangled Up Over There

If you cross Queens Boulevard
ten thousand times in a single day you
might get hit by a delivery van carrying

a veggie pizza and diet coke to Clippings-
n-Cuts on Austin Street where Harold
the hairdresser theorizes about whether

anything can be done in Syria and
Iraq where people lop off heads to
get their points across when they

could chop off hair instead and not
bloody the desert floor with human
gore, which makes Harold sore we're

involved in that part of the world when it
was the British and French that caused the
split ends by cutting the Ottoman Empire

into counterfeit countries after World War One,
shaving tribesmen from their local regions,
coloring opinion against the new rulers,

adding layers of problems, permanent waves to an
already difficult do that if England and France had
not restyled would have been better for America

because it's all tangled up over there.

Oblivious

Goodness in the Gilded Age

A stockbroker bumped into the
   good-deed fairy on the E train.
She was wearing a short frilly dress,

holding a pink magic wand, and
   sporting gossamer wings flecked with
glittering faith and selfless delight.

He apologized for accidentally
   banging into her. She replied no
apology needed, give a dollar to the

homeless guy with the frayed black
   pants, tattered sneakers, and tattooed
allegories on his arms sitting at the

bottom of the uptown staircase in the
   Broadway-Lafayette Station with a
cardboard sign around his neck saying

I am drowning in a sea of grief. The
   broker smiled wryly at the charitable
apparition, adjusted his Rolex, buttoned

his blazer, and focused his thoughts on
   the presentation he would be giving
later in the day to the piggies at the

bank on the near-term outlook for
   pork belly options.

Waiting

Sunday on a Bench

She is sitting next to
me reading *21 Ways to
Happiness and Peace* / says
her husband's been sick a
long time / Recon Marine /
Vietnam /Agent Orange / three
heart attacks / lupus / cancer /
always upbeat / optimistic /
unlike Pop she says / furious at
being ill / having her care for
him / feeding tubes / incontinence /
her nights are bad / days are better
/ suicide's a tempting thought / but
she'll be strong / believes in Jesus /
sure that he will get her through /
my wife rings up / I have to go /
to pick up food / sorry I can't
stay some more / nice meeting
you / she says to me / hope you
have a blessed day / I wish her well /
and say the same / drive off to do
the crying.

Getting and Spending

America the Dutiful

Bargain hunters running
　'round the mall on a rainy
　　Fourth of Good Buys

shopping for men's apparel,
　women's apparel, furniture,
　　shoes, chocolate, sports gear,

jewelry, household appliances,
　cell phones, novelty gifts bought
　　and brought to the food court

where nutrition is done on
　the cheap and thoughts of
　　what's on sale are good reason

to not call mom
　or pay a visit to dad.

Fenced

Rally 'Round the Flag

Let's rally 'round the flag
blowing larger than life,
bigger than death, in

oil-engorged, blood-swelled
desert climes where blown-up
cars and bloated corpses lie

far from the malls and stalls
of suburban shopping centers
where teenagers worry about

dimples and pimples and
sneakers and jeans.

I'll charter a bus from
World War II to put us in
a patriotic, V for victory,

we're-all-in-this-together
frame of mind and we can
croon America the Beautiful,

The Star-Spangled Banner, and
Ninety-nine Bottles of Beer on
the Wall as we go barreling down

a pothole, out of control, no goal
highway littered with wreckage
from Korea, Vietnam, Iraq,

Afghanistan—brutal futile feuds
that looked aces at the start but
turned into fold 'em don't hold

'em and let's not embolden the

rest of the world from messing
with us.

Don't forget to wear your
John Wayne *Life is Tough,
Tougher if You're Stupid*

T-shirt and your *Love It or
Leave It* baseball cap with
the map of the USA sewn in

Three-D, Day-Glo, way to go
my country right or wrong to
the demonstration.

And don't forget war is
hellacious but goodness
gracious it makes for

dynamic discussions 'round the
water cooler and gives us something
to think about besides a lousy

economy, global warming, and
tales told by two-faced politicians
full of sound and fury

signifying zilch.

How Much?

Nine Dead in Dayton

Nine dead in Dayton,
twenty-two in El Paso,
twenty-one in San Ysidro,
fourteen in San Bernardino,

fifty-eight by a Las Vegas casino,
a crowd of concertgoers,
bodies lying bleeding, a
nation that is reeling, the

core of who we are, posting
hate, loading up, firing fast
and down they go in Walmarts,
at festivals, inside of schools,

inside of bars, one hundred
rounds a minute, death is a
democracy, knows no color,
knows no sex, equality for all;

bullets pierce pliant flesh,
splinter bones, don't tread on
me the gun nuts say, Columbine,
Parkland, Sandy Hook, Aurora,

thoughts and prayers,
fictitious care, death
and dying everywhere.

Coney Island Dreaming

Brooklyn 1957

Eleven years old, lost in Prospect Park
   with my friend Alan Weberman, a beatnik
who doesn't play stickball, stoopball, or shoot
   water pistols but wears French berets, black
turtleneck sweaters and bangs the bongos.

We're trying to find a way out of a
   585-acre urban wilderness in the
heart of deepest Brooklyn with
   no maps, canteens, compass,
food, or shining stars to guide us.

We're far from Sol's candy store
   with its vanilla egg creams, chocolate
Clark Bars, Drake's pound cakes,
   cherry lime rickeys and long salted
pretzels in glass see-through bins.

We're far from the Patio Movie Theater,
   with its double features, cartoons,
newsreels, and a beautifully tiled lobby
   with a goldfish pond to throw pennies in.

We're far from Jahn's Ice Cream Parlor with
   its Kitchen Sink—a jumble of ice cream,
chocolate syrup, whipped cream, maraschino
   cherries, and a hodgepodge of other things
that can serve up to six.

We're far from the Empire Rollerdrome,
   Ebinger's Bakery, Erasmus Hall High School,
Freddie Fitzsimmons Bowling Lanes, and
   Ebbets Field, home of the '55 world champs,
'57 world chumps, who left Flatbush for LA.

We're far from college, marriage,
   work, retirement, and a quiet
home in the country to look back on
   the racket, hubbub, and delight
of inner-city childhood life.

Keep Stepping

Rock Around the Clock

The hit single version of *Rock
Around the Clock* was not the
one used in *The Blackboard
Jungle*, a flic filled with
delinquent teens, brass
knuckles, and rebel rock
played on *American
Bandstand* with its
lip-sync recording artists,
autograph sessions, the
latest dance fads, a fab
afternoon TV-lineup that
featured Kenny, Arlene and
the other Bandstand kids doing
the Shake, the Madison and the
Stroll, which were helpful for
picking up girls at parties before
or after Spin the Bottle when
you had ten seconds to kiss and
if the time was up you had to
French kiss which wasn't that bad
even if your partner wore braces
and didn't know that Chuck Berry
would soon be in jail, Little Richard
would become a preacher, and Elvis
would get drafted into the army.

"Just desserts" said my parents who
preferred Lawrence Welk, Bing
Crosby, and Patti Page to a bunch of
bad boys playing Satan's music,
so I turned up the collar of my
black leather jacket, put a little
dab of Brylcreem on my hair,
dropped some dimes in a diner
jukebox and blasted my transistor

radio through the 'hood.

I was invincible, indestructible,
unconquerable, impregnable,
then the plane crash, Buddy Holly,
Ritchie Valens, The Big Bopper,
the Third of February 1959,
"the day the music died," but
not for me, not for the with-it kids
who scrambled into the sixties.

Hendrix, Joplin, protests, a
Summer of Love. Led Zeppelin,
a decade later, buying a stairway
to heaven we all wanted to climb.

Nothing Left to See

This is the Way the World Ends

A blackened dove with hardly
any feathers flew past my window
today before crashing wildly to earth,
the start of the seventh extinction.

Adios fish tacos and chicken fajitas
@ Antojitos de Michoacan. Au revoir
movies, museums, and remembrance
of things past.

It's been a great ride through the rodeo of
everyday existence and it ends with a bang
not a whimper; irreconcilable grievances,
nuclear annihilation,

That's one small step for man,
one giant leap for Armageddon.

As the cockroaches crawl amidst
debris from verbal bombast and
moral braggadocio, the people
who remain march wordlessly
into the abyss.

Getting Through

Covid-19

Bad news wrapped in a protein /
a cellular saboteur / a biological
Chernobyl exploding in a
leaderless land / triage tents /
portable morgues / blue latex
gloves on a city street / the virus
kills / it screams you must change
your life / Zoom consoles but
touch is above technology / a
doctor cries "We need more
beds, protective gear / no one
wants to die alone / there's
no way out but THROUGH."

MIND AND NATURE

Ponder on the Rock

First Thought, Best Thought

First thought, best thought,
worked for Allen Ginsberg.
Work for me?
Let's see.

If a tree fell in the forest and
killed you would it make a
sound when it hit the ground?
What kind of sound? A simile,
a metaphor, an allusion, a contusion?

If Godot showed up early
and was waiting for you,
what would you tell him?
What would you do?

Can a liar be true to his own self?
Can a slow rolling stone gather moss?
If you are late to bed and late to rise
can you still be healthy, wealthy,
and wise?

Were the good old days all that good?
Are you really so badly misunderstood?
If you removed Latin expressions from
the law would lawyers lose their power
to over awe?

First thought, best thought
best thought, less thought
less thought, next thought
next thought, pigeon pie.

New Dawn

On Reaching Seventy

I want to be a super-ager
like the sun, bright and
badass in the morning,

blazing hot through the day,
kicking sand up at the moon
that sedately stays in place while

le soleil heads for the horizon to
lift weights, do curls in a
celestial gym where planets

jog around their orbits,
galaxies stretch and asteroids spot
comets under their frozen cores

as they shoot through space
thinking they're faster than
old-man sol 'cause they got

slim solar-system bodies
and dust and gas ion tails
that may look good to the

casual observer but aren't
well suited for warming up
the atmosphere or keeping

the Earth going, tasks
Mister Bright Star
shines in.

Woodland Friend

Who's Listening

I talk to the trees but
they never listen to me.
Ditto, the stars and
the breeze. Hey, if
you can't talk to
yourself who can
you talk with. Just
don't forget who's
listening.

Trunk Trick

A Mammoth Lamentation

You trip over my trunk,
get hit by my tail,
crash into my legs,
are nicked by my tusks,
yet you act as
if I'm not there.

What have I done to deserve
such scorn and contempt? Why
am I the pariah at the party?

I've got feelings and they get hurt
when you don't acknowledge
my existence, to wit,

Johnny's a drug addict,
Mary's cheating on her husband,
Ralph didn't die of old age.

Is it so hard to admit that
population growth threatens
the planet, that war is good for

business, that democracy is
not a perfect system, that
climate change is real?

I don't need encomiums or
compliments, just some candor
and a little sincerity that will

keep me from becoming the
emperor's new clothes,
an 800-pound gorilla,

a woebegone elephant
trapped in a room.

Energy Matters

The Formula E=mc²

The formula $E=mc^2$ basically states
if you can convert a small amount of
matter *completely* it will yield a
huge amount of energy.

Well I'm no Einstein but I know doing
anything completely is pretty damn hard
unless it's completely forgetting where
you put your car keys.

As for producing huge amounts of
energy, go to a Knicks game, watch
those suckers play. Jeering from the
crowd could power a hydroelectric plant.

Or ask my upstairs neighbor to turn
down her TV. Vitriol that will spew
from her rosy red lips could run a
nuclear sub for a couple of years.

Then there's the speed of light,
the c in the equation. If you could
journey at 186,000 miles per second
you'd just wind up watching more TV
in the hotel when you got there.

People shouldn't worry so much
about changing mass, moving fast.
We should all just slow down, read a

good book, see a
good movie, have a
good meal, and be
good to each other.

From All Over

Labels

I am a jigsaw puzzle with bent and
broken pieces that if dropped in a

therapist's office would scatter its
social construction and fall into a

multicultural mélange that emerged
about 200,000 years ago in East Africa

and spread through Eurasia, Oceania, and
the Americas, feeding and interbreeding,

speaking thousands of different languages,
framing the world in ways Charles Darwin

and Walt Whitman would say are both
unique and commonplace and not easily

categorized by checking a box on a
census form.

Crème Brûlée, Etc...

C'est la Vie

A woman in a black dress eats a
tarte flambée in a French bistro on
a rainy afternoon in New York City.
Across from her table my friend and I

share salmon en croûte, a potato omelet,
views on how nuclear proliferation,
overpopulation and global warming
are killing the planet as the crawl on

the video screen above the bar cycles
stories about African Ebola and
racial strife in the USA. My friend
says his sister has just moved to

New York from LA. I tell him
my wife wants out of the Big Apple,
a place I love as much as the woman
in black loves the crème brûlée she

orders to go which she offers to share
with us but we're full and invite her to
have a drink she declines because she has
to leave to care for a sick child at home.

Enchanted Forest

Lost in Thought

Lost in thought
in thickets and birds
flowers and trees
sun overhead
no clouds in the sky
and wouldn't you know it
I've tripped
on a branch
I should have seen
if I hadn't been thinking
I should have been
quiet and listened to you
when you told me to get
waffles at Key Food
two cans of soup
frozen burritos
don't forget cheese
and cold cuts for lunch
instead of replying
I'm not forgetful
you think I am stupid
just tell me the items
you want me to get
then into the car
and off to the woods
where I'm taking a walk
and thinking real hard
was it four cans of soup
and what did you say
we needed for lunch?

Mixed Use

Along the Peconic

I'd rather read the papers than
   write this poem for I can't think of
anything to say and the yard needs
   mowing, the car needs washing, the

tub needs scrubbing, and I guess
   I'll make myself a cup of coffee,
have a bit of the scone I bought
   this morning at Briermere Farms

after the finish of a four-mile stroll
   along the banks of the Peconic
where I watched a vesper sparrow
   circle lazy in the sky, a stratocumulus

cloud hang low on the horizon, a
   teal blue kayak drift leisurely past
a McDonald's parking lot that abuts
   the water upon which floated a white

plastic coffee lid and two cigarette stubs
   that seemed horribly out of place in
a place where fluke, flounder, and
   striped bass hail from, and swans,

gulls, geese, and Carolina ducks
   also call home.

Time to Turn Back

Summer's End

A crescent beach, seashells,
lapidary waves. I walk past
couples lying on the sand
glistening with oil and good
intentions.

I turn my head to catch the
breeze and watch fishermen
going out to sea in rickety
boats, eating, laughing,
drinking beer.

Marching home through the
woods a deer bounds across
my path full of health and
vigor I no longer possess
but can't help yearning for.

I make my way toward
a bungalow facing the
Pine Barrens where a family
of five wild turkeys ambles
across my lawn.

A pair of jays as blue as the sky
in spring fly in and out of the
Americana two-hole birdhouse
I built last year. A mailman
deposits letters inside my green

galvanized steel, post mounted
mailbox. Orange and purple
dahlias planted a month ago
finally coming into bloom. The
sprinkler goes round and round.

My neighbor across the way
brings over beefsteak tomatoes
just harvested from his yard,
invites me by for barbequed

hot dogs, burgers, corn,
potato salad, watermelon,
homemade apple pie.

He asks when I'm
returning to the city.

I want to say never.

But I don't.

Sail

The Penitent Sea

A sea is a large body of salt water
   surrounded in whole or in part
by land and the projections of
   beach walkers who stare into

the roiling surf and see friends that
   disappoint, jobs that didn't work out,
a world gone awry due to climate
   change, terrorism, poverty, and

sorry I forgot it was your birthday,
   not a hanging crime except in the
State of Perfection where everyone
   remembers everything and nothing

falls through the cracks which is
   an utter impossibility due to
faulty human wiring that leads
   people to screw up from time to

time: Pearl Harbor, Hurricane Katrina,
   the twelve book publishers
who turned down Harry Potter,
   the fourteen relatives I offended

when I showed up a day late for
   my family reunion and said
life is an adventure in forgiveness,
   a quest for clemency, a search for

absolution, a mix of metaphor
   mornings and makeshift afternoons
where the sea surges and laughs at
   the errors I make.

Warm Waters

Every Day is Earth Day

Every day is Earth Day for
seven billion human beings,
one to ten trillion trees, eight
point seven million species that

celebrate and suffer existence
and maybe a day at the beach
with Aunt Rita and her little red
tote bag packed with tuna wraps

and apples for a noon time lunch
while gill-bearing aquatic
creatures seek provender of a
different sort, dolphins and

porpoises cavort lazily in the
undulating waves, a polar bear
paddles in the Arctic Ocean to
find a stable ice floe, a camel

naps, perchance to dream, in
the largest hot desert in the
world, a cockroach crawls
across a teak-stained hardwood

floor in an Amsterdam coffee shop
as an Andean condor scans the
coast for carrion over Tierra del
Fuego and a Tasmanian devil

eats a dying wombat hit by a car
alongside a road in Australia.
In the Bay of Fundy a ferry
founders killing all on board.

But three hundred eighty-five
thousand babies come into the
world each day and the tides
roll in and the tides roll out

and life goes on.

Do Not Disturb

Wish Me Good Luck

Wish me good luck as I write this damn thing,
A challenging task on a bright sunny day
When a walk in the woods is beckoning me
To leave my desk chair and writerly cares
And amble on paths to contemplate nature
And dream of good work that simply gets done.

But nothing is simple in getting work done,
Though such a belief is a comforting thing,
For it seems to be in my basic nature
If I think a chore can be through in a day
I don't fret and add gratuitous cares
That would cause me to whine woe is me,

Woe is me, woe is me, woe is me.
Repetition in writing is easily done,
It lessens the burden of prosodic cares.
A thing is a thing is a thing is a thing,
Thinging like that just makes my day.
Ah nature, ah nature, ah nature, ah nature.

And did I not mention ah nature, ah nature?
And let me throw in woe is me, woe is me.
Oh, jubilant day, jubilant day,
This sestina is rolling and round the bend done.
Recap and reprise are truly the thing
To banish and vanish authorial cares.

Authorial cares, authorial cares,
Most natural but not existing in nature
Where symbols are not the primary things.
But symbols are crucial to people like me,
I use words in my poems, *dats how dey get done*,
I pray this one over by end of the day,

By end of the day, by end of the day

I hope all my dread cares, yes all my dread cares,
Will cease and this job will be finally done.
I'm impelled and incited by my inner nature,
Which seems to be pressing and pushing at me
To do this darn thing, to do this darn thing, this thing

That keeps me from trekking the woods, this thing
That keeps me from trekking the woods, keeps me
From trekking the beautiful woods, pricks my impetuous nature.

Levels of Abstraction

Ode to the Structural Differential

I hail Alfred Korzybski's physical model
of reality in which a disc and suitcase-
shaped tags show that I abstract from
my environments, that there is a
sub-atomic domain beyond my
direct observation, that what
I experience I can not fully
describe, and that there
is more to heaven
and earth than
is contained
in my verbal
philosophy.

www.ingramcontent.com/pod-product-compliance
Lightning Source LLC
Chambersburg PA
CBHW040211260925
33201CB00024B/2184